TWENTY–YEARS OF U.S. POLICY ON NORTH KOREA: FROM AGREED FRAMEWORK TO STRATEGIC PATIENCE

HEARING

BEFORE THE

SUBCOMMITTEE ON ASIA AND THE PACIFIC

OF THE

COMMITTEE ON FOREIGN AFFAIRS
HOUSE OF REPRESENTATIVES

ONE HUNDRED THIRTEENTH CONGRESS

SECOND SESSION

JULY 30, 2014

Serial No. 113–214

Printed for the use of the Committee on Foreign Affairs

Available via the World Wide Web: http://www.foreignaffairs.house.gov/ or
http://www.gpo.gov/fdsys/

U.S. GOVERNMENT PRINTING OFFICE

88–917PDF   WASHINGTON : 2014

For sale by the Superintendent of Documents, U.S. Government Printing Office
Internet: bookstore.gpo.gov   Phone: toll free (866) 512–1800; DC area (202) 512–1800
Fax: (202) 512–2104   Mail: Stop IDCC, Washington, DC 20402–0001

COMMITTEE ON FOREIGN AFFAIRS

EDWARD R. ROYCE, California, *Chairman*

CHRISTOPHER H. SMITH, New Jersey
ILEANA ROS-LEHTINEN, Florida
DANA ROHRABACHER, California
STEVE CHABOT, Ohio
JOE WILSON, South Carolina
MICHAEL T. McCAUL, Texas
TED POE, Texas
MATT SALMON, Arizona
TOM MARINO, Pennsylvania
JEFF DUNCAN, South Carolina
ADAM KINZINGER, Illinois
MO BROOKS, Alabama
TOM COTTON, Arkansas
PAUL COOK, California
GEORGE HOLDING, North Carolina
RANDY K. WEBER SR., Texas
SCOTT PERRY, Pennsylvania
STEVE STOCKMAN, Texas
RON DeSANTIS, Florida
DOUG COLLINS, Georgia
MARK MEADOWS, North Carolina
TED S. YOHO, Florida
SEAN DUFFY, Wisconsin
CURT CLAWSON, Florida

ELIOT L. ENGEL, New York
ENI F.H. FALEOMAVAEGA, American
 Samoa
BRAD SHERMAN, California
GREGORY W. MEEKS, New York
ALBIO SIRES, New Jersey
GERALD E. CONNOLLY, Virginia
THEODORE E. DEUTCH, Florida
BRIAN HIGGINS, New York
KAREN BASS, California
WILLIAM KEATING, Massachusetts
DAVID CICILLINE, Rhode Island
ALAN GRAYSON, Florida
JUAN VARGAS, California
BRADLEY S. SCHNEIDER, Illinois
JOSEPH P. KENNEDY III, Massachusetts
AMI BERA, California
ALAN S. LOWENTHAL, California
GRACE MENG, New York
LOIS FRANKEL, Florida
TULSI GABBARD, Hawaii
JOAQUIN CASTRO, Texas

AMY PORTER, *Chief of Staff*   THOMAS SHEEHY, *Staff Director*
JASON STEINBAUM, *Democratic Staff Director*

SUBCOMMITTEE ON ASIA AND THE PACIFIC

STEVE CHABOT, Ohio, *Chairman*

DANA ROHRABACHER, California
MATT SALMON, Arizona
MO BROOKS, Alabama
GEORGE HOLDING, North Carolina
SCOTT PERRY, Pennsylvania
DOUG COLLINS, Georgia
CURT CLAWSON, Florida

ENI F.H. FALEOMAVAEGA, American
 Samoa
AMI BERA, California
TULSI GABBARD, Hawaii
BRAD SHERMAN, California
GERALD E. CONNOLLY, Virginia
WILLIAM KEATING, Massachusetts

CONTENTS

Page

WITNESSES

The Honorable Glyn Davies, Special Representative for North Korea Policy, Bureau of East Asian and Pacific Affairs, U.S. Department of State 6
The Honorable Robert King, Special Envoy for North Korean Human Rights, Office of the Special Envoy for Human Rights in North Korea, U.S. Department of State 14

LETTERS, STATEMENTS, ETC., SUBMITTED FOR THE HEARING

The Honorable Glyn Davies: Prepared statement 8
The Honorable Robert King: Prepared statement 16

APPENDIX

Hearing notice..36
Hearing minutes...37

(III)

TWENTY–YEARS OF U.S. POLICY ON NORTH KOREA: FROM AGREED FRAMEWORK TO STRATEGIC PATIENCE

WEDNESDAY, JULY 30, 2014

House of Representatives,
Subcommittee on Asia and the Pacific,
Committee on Foreign Affairs,
Washington, DC.

The committee met, pursuant to notice, at 2 o'clock p.m., in room 2172 Rayburn House Office Building, Hon. Steve Chabot (chairman of the subcommittee) presiding.

Mr. CHABOT. Good afternoon and welcome to this afternoon's subcommittee hearing. I want to thank Mr. Ami Bera for serving as today's ranking member and also thank our distinguished witnesses for being here. It has taken 6 months for our schedules to align, so we hope this afternoon's hearing is a productive one.

In March, this subcommittee held a hearing to examine the findings of the United Nations Commission of Inquiry Report on human rights in North Korea. Anyone would be hard pressed to deny the extent of human rights abuses being committed by the most repressive totalitarian regime on earth. The report, the first of its kind, was a shocking wake-up call for the international community to take action—for the U.S. to take action. Unfortunately, it's been over 5 months and we're still waiting for some pretty significant action on this.

North Korea is one of the greatest security threats to the peace and stability of Asia and one of the United States' most vexing security challenges. It is also one of the greatest policy failures of the past two decades.

This year marks the 20th anniversary since the United States and North Korea signed the Agreed Framework, which called on North Korea to freeze operation and construction of nuclear reactors suspected of being part of a covert nuclear weapons program. While this agreement framed our relations for about 8 years, from North Korea's vantage point it was a ruse, as the entire time Pyongyang continued to develop its uranium-enrichment capabilities.

Then, in an effort to continue nuclear negotiations with North Korea, we took a multilateral approach and began the Six-Party Talks. Once again, concession after concession, this method of negotiation also failed and has been stalled since December 2008.

So where are we today? North Korea has tested three nuclear devices since 2006, the most recent in early 2013, and has declared itself a nuclear armed state. Belligerent and threatening rhetoric from Pyongyang's dilettante leader has escalated since he took the Kim throne in December 2011. It has launched nearly 100 ballistic missiles, artillery and rockets combined since the beginning of this year. And its web of illicit activities and dealings with terrorist organizations around the world has expanded. Ultimately, North Korea's proliferation of nuclear weapons and support to groups that oppose Western interests continues unfettered and without limitation.

Most of the world's attention today is locked on Ukraine, where Russia is supporting the infiltration of rebel troops into Crimea and Eastern Ukraine; and the Middle East, where Hamas operatives in Gaza are trying to wipe Israel off the map. But we must also look East. It should come as no surprise that just this past weekend, it was reported that Hamas militants are negotiating a weapons deal worth hundreds of thousands of dollars with North Korea for missiles and communications equipment. This relationship was first made public in 2009 when 35 tons of surface-to-surface rockets and rocket-propelled grenades were destined for Iran, which then planned to smuggle to Hezbollah in Lebanon and Hamas in Gaza. And last week, a U.S. Federal judge ruled that North Korea, in concert with Iran and Syria, was responsible for providing materials and assistance to Hezbollah terrorists who fired rockets into Israel during an offense that occurred in 2006. But again, nothing is being done to obstruct these weapons sales or the cargo ships traversing the world's oceans with weapons in the cargo bay.

Over the years, North Korea has branded itself as a one-stop shop for missile and nuclear materials and technology—the ultimate facilitating bad guy—providing whatever its anti-American friends want so long as it gets the oil, cash and materials it needs to maintain the power of the Kim regime. It is not a secret that North Korea has long cavorted with the likes of Iran and Syria, and in fact helped build Syria's nuclear facility destroyed by Israel in 2007. North Korea's last nuclear test, where Iranian nuclear experts were reportedly present, also underlined the harsh reality— North Korea's weapons capabilities are advanced and possibly more advanced than Iran's, further highlighting the tremendous failure of efforts made by every administration since the early 1990s.

As the evidence continues to mount of the grave threat that North Korea poses to the rest of the world, the Obama administration's official position is that North Korea is ''not known to have sponsored any terrorist acts since the bombing of a Korean Airline's flight in 1987.'' Even more staggering, on July 20th, Secretary Kerry noted that North Korea was ''quieter'' than previous years and that the U.S. is indeed ''moving forward'' with efforts to denuclearize North Korea. According to our records, the past few months have been one of the most historically active periods by North Korea in terms of testing missiles, including U.N. restricted ballistic technology. I don't think North Korea's recent behavior can be called ''quiet.''

Simply put, the administration's do nothing "strategic patience policy" is crumbling to pieces waiting for North Korea to beseech for negotiations aimed at limiting its nuclear and missile potential. Kim Jong-un has no interest in denuclearization. Outsourcing our North Korea policy to China, North Korea's top trading partner and source of revenue, has also yielded little progress, but we are still sitting idly by, waiting for Beijing's patience with Pyongyang to wear thin.

The ongoing pursuit of restarting Six-Party Talks is futile. It has been 6 years and at this point, we are only wasting time as Pyongyang augments its fissile material stockpile and improves its missile and nuclear capabilities. The administration refuses to impose tougher and more targeted sanctions on North Korea like those on Russia, Zimbabwe, Iran, Cuba, Sudan, and Belarus because it believes doing so would "unnecessarily hinder its ability to conduct foreign policy." It won't list the world's most prolific money launderer, counterfeiter, and state drug trafficker as a country of Primary Money Laundering Concern, but Iran and Burma are; and our current policy has done nothing to help the North Korean people. I remain disappointed that so little has been done to hold the Kim regime responsible for its horrific human rights abuses detailed in the U.N. Commission of Inquiry Report.

North Korea is a grave threat to the United States and our allies in Asia. We cannot continue to wait for North Korea to decide it wants to negotiate. A non-nuclear North Korea is an elusive goal if the administration maintains its current strategic trajectory. The Kim regime is responsible for the horrific deaths of people not only within North Korea, but around the world. It is time to put our resources together and act. Rewarding North Korea for "reversible steps" on the pretense that it will commit to denuclearization has failed before, so let us not "buy the same horse twice."

I look forward to hearing from our witnesses and I yield to the ranking member, Mr. Bera, for 5 minutes.

Mr. BERA. Thank you, Chairman Chabot. Thank you for calling this important hearing. I also want to thank the witnesses today for your service to our country and your patience in what has to be one of the most diplomatic challenges in terms of moving North Korea forward.

As mentioned, this year marks the 20th anniversary of the agreed framework between the United States and North Korea. Our foreign policy toward North Korea has always been challenging, given that North Korea's posture in the region is inconsistent and at times aggressive. That said, throughout the years we have tried on numerous occasions to negotiate with North Korea on denuclearization, while also promoting the strategic patience approach. However, I continue to be very concerned, as the chairman has mentioned, with North Korea's nuclear ambitions, its aggression toward our allies in South Korea and Japan, and its dismal human rights record.

North Korea's testing of ballistic missiles and nuclear tests throughout the last 15 years is unacceptable and poses serious security concerns in the region. Earlier this month, North Korea fired more than 100 rockets and artillery shells toward South Korea's border presumably in protest of joint U.S. and South Korean military exercises. And our allies in Japan, even as they attempt to promote diplomatic dialogue with North Korea on resolving the abductions of Japanese citizens, the Korean People's Army launched short-range missiles into the Sea of Japan in late June. These type of provocative actions toward our allies are deeply concerning. The U.S.-China relationship, along with our trilateral relations with South Korea and Japan is crucial in solving the inter-Korean conflict. We have to take an original approach and we have to work together with our partners in the region.

The conflict has multilateral implications and therefore is not only a U.S. interest. As the world's greatest democracy, we must take a tougher stance with the international community on North Korea's threatening antics. North Korea must view our partnership as a regional effort to support a peaceful and stable Pacific region. We have to put the pressure on the North Korean Government with stricter sanctions so we can engage in diplomatic dialogue and make positive steps toward denuclearization. We should also encourage North Korea to enforce the 2005 Six-Party Talk agreements. North Korea should be sincere with its commitment to the 2005 joint statement and allow IAEA inspectors to renew their activity in the country.

I am also concerned with North Korea's deplorable human rights record. North Koreans do not have freedom of speech, movement, or religion and are also subject to chronic starvation and a dismal public health system. The U.S., based on our values as Americans, should remain a strong supporter and leader within the global community in promoting human rights.

I look forward to reviewing our actions, positions, and policies toward North Korea as we work on denuclearization and our human rights record. Mr. Chairman, with that, I would like to yield back and thank you for calling this hearing.

Mr. CHABOT. Thank you, the gentleman yields. The gentleman from California is recognized for an opening statement.

Mr. SHERMAN. Thank you, Mr. King, welcome home. Mr. Chairman, thank you for holding these hearings. It was just a few months ago that you and I were at the DMZ and also discussing North Korea with President Park and with Prime Minister Abe. North Korea doesn't trade with us, doesn't need us. It needs China from which it obtains enormous subsidies. We should be trying to change the behavior of North Korea directly and more importantly China with a combination of carrots and sticks, even though the North Korean Government is despicable and politically we could all try to outdo each other and who could be more opposed to the government, both carrots and sticks are called for.

On the carrot side, we ought to discuss with North Korea a non-aggression pact. They have asked for that in the past. It isn't our usual way of conducting State Department business, but it is something they want, something we can give them. And if they ever see that Mr. Cheney might be Vice President again, they might appreciate an official U.S. position against invasion.

Second, we can tell the Chinese that even if there is unification, no American military forces will be stationed north of the 38th parallel.

As to sticks, we have to look at the lopsided trade relationship with China, access to the U.S. markets is not guaranteed by the U.N. charter. North Korea may not be quite as dangerous as other states because it is not as ambitious as Iran. It seeks only to oppress its own people. But with a erratic government shown to be even more erratic in the last 6 months, and a growing nuclear stockpile, we have ever reason to try to trim the danger posed by North Korea. I yield back.

Mr. CHABOT. Thank you. The gentleman yields back. I would now like to introduce our distinguished panel here this afternoon. Ambassador Glyn Davies is the Special Representative of the Secretary of State for North Korean policy. He was appointed in January 2012 to facilitate high-level engagement with our other Six-Party Talk partners. He serves as a senior emissary for U.S. engagement with North Korea. He also oversees U.S. involvement in the Six-Party Talks process, as well as other aspects of our security, political, economic, human rights, and humanitarian assistance policy regarding North Korea.

Special Representative Davies is a career member of the Senior Foreign Service and served as the Permanent Representative of the United States to the International Atomic Energy Agency and the United Nations office in Vienna. His prior assignments include Principal Deputy Assistant Secretary of State, Bureau of East Asian and Pacific Affairs and Executive Secretary of the National Security Council staff and we welcome you this afternoon, Mr. Ambassador.

I will next introduce Robert King. Ambassador Robert King became the Special Envoy for North Korean Human Rights Issues in November 2009 following confirmation by the United States Senate. Ambassador King works under Ambassador Davies and has the lead on human rights and humanitarian affairs. Prior to his appointment, Ambassador King worked on Capitol Hill for 25 years—24 of those years as chief of staff to Congressman Tom Lantos. He was concurrently staff director of the Foreign Affairs Committee of the U.S. House of Representatives, Democratic staff director of the committee, and held various professional staff positions on the committee since 1993. Ambassador King holds a Ph.D. in International Relations from the Fletcher School of Law and Diplomacy, Tufts University. He has authored several books and numerous articles on international relations and we welcome you here this afternoon as well, Mr. Ambassador.

I am sure you are both familiar with the 5-minute rule so I won't take a lot of time. The yellow light will come on and it means you have 1 minute and we hope you wrap up as close as possible when the red light comes on and we will limit ourselves to 5 minutes as well.

We will begin with you, Ambassador Davies. You are recognized for 5 minutes.

STATEMENT OF THE HONORABLE GLYN DAVIES, SPECIAL REPRESENTATIVE FOR NORTH KOREA POLICY, BUREAU OF EAST ASIAN AND PACIFIC AFFAIRS, U.S. DEPARTMENT OF STATE

Mr. DAVIES. Chairman Chabot, thanks so much. Representative Bera, and members of the committee, thanks so much for inviting me and my colleague, Ambassador King, to testify today on U.S. policy toward the Democratic People's Republic of Korea, DPRK for short, commonly known as North Korea.

The North Korean regime is a global pariah. It works against the interests of its own people, its neighbors, and the world.

Mr. CHABOT. Would you mind pulling the mic just a little bit closer?

Mr. DAVIES. Sure, absolutely.

Mr. CHABOT. I want everybody in the room to hear.

Mr. DAVIES. Here we go, is that better?

Mr. CHABOT. That is better.

Mr. DAVIES. It violates its obligations by pursuing nuclear weapons and ballistic missiles, posing a growing threat to the United States, our friends and allies, and the global nonproliferation regime. It devotes an enormous amount of its scarce resources to weapons, to a massive standing army, and to vanity projects, all while nine out of ten North Koreans suffer.

We have no illusions about the nature of the regime. We have refused to reward its provocations with concessions. We have instead tightened sanctions and told the DPRK that neither its occasional charm offenses nor its more frequent aggressive behavior will lead us to accept a nuclear armed North Korea. Like all recent administrations, we are open to engagement when possible, but will apply pressure as needed.

Despite DPRK backtracking, we remain committed to authentic and credible denuclearization talks, but talks won't succeed until Pyongyang recognizes and demonstrates that it will live up to its promises. Regrettably, the DPRK increasingly rejects meaningful negotiations. Instead, it has unleashed multiple provocations that have drawn condemnation and increased its isolation. Just in recent weeks, it has conducted repeated ballistic missile launches in violation of U.N. Security Council resolutions. These followed similar launches earlier this spring, punctuated on March 30 with threats to conduct a new type of nuclear test.

The DPRK says it wants talks without preconditions. Translation: It seeks open-ended Six-Party Talks to gain acceptance as a nuclear weapons state, and to camouflage its secret weapons development. We are not interested in talks unless their primary order of business is implementing North Korea's September 2005 promise to denuclearize.

The Republic of Korea is squarely at the center of our efforts. There is no daylight between us on what we expect from North Korea. President Obama, speaking in South Korea in April, expressed support for President Park's vision of peaceful, progressive unification. The U.S.-ROK alliance in its 60th year is stronger than ever. Our day-to-day combined efforts to maintain peace and stability on the peninsular send a strong deterrence signal to North Korea that the security it seeks is not to be found in nuclear weapons. Our growing U.S.-ROK-Japan trilateral security cooperation also sends a powerful message of deterrence to Pyongyang.

As North Korea's last remaining protector and patron, China, has a key role to play in convincing North Korea to denuclearize. That is why North Korea remains at the top of our bilateral agenda with Beijing. Secretary Kerry raised it prominently there in early July.

We welcome the steps that PRC has taken to oppose Pyongyang's nuclear weapons program. Since 2012, China has voted for two new rounds of U.N. sanctions and last year, published a 900 item control list banning their export to North Korea. Together with our allies and partners, we seek to show North Korea its nuclear program stands in the way of the secure future it says it wants. We continue to increase the cost of its illicit activities by unilaterally tightening sanctions. We work closely with the U.N. Security Council and like-minded partners to ensure full implementation of the four key Security Council resolutions.

The July 2013 seizure by Panama of a huge cache of military gear demonstrates U.N. sanctions are effective.

The welfare of North Korea's people is an essential focus of U.S. policy. The vast majority suffer from the Government's self-impoverishing military-first policy. The U.N. Commission of Inquiry's sobering report detailed the systematic, widespread, and gross human rights violations being committed by the DPRK.

My colleague, Robert King's tireless efforts for many years demonstrate that human rights is a constant focus for us. There are three U.S. citizens that are being held by North Korea. Their continued detention is a serious stumbling block to approved U.S.-DPRK relations. We will continue to advocate for their freedom and thank Congress for its steadfast support in these efforts.

Mr. Chairman, we aim to convince the DPRK to comply with its obligations, end its isolation, and respect of the rights of its people. Each outrageous North Korean act discredits the assertion it is driven to act belligerently by others' hostility. It is now clearer than ever that North Korea is developing nuclear weapons and ballistic missiles merely to prolong the Kim regime and to obtain benefits from the international community. North Korea alone is responsible for North Korean actions and resolving the DPRK nuclear program is a multilateral task.

Just as North Korea's original aggression against the South was met with a strong response from the United Nations, standing up to North Korea today requires a concerted effort by the entire international community.

Thank you again, Mr. Chairman, and members of the panel for the opportunity to appear before you today and I am happy, obviously, to take your questions.

[The prepared statement of Mr. Davies follows:]

Testimony of Glyn T. Davies
Special Representative for North Korea Policy
U.S. Department of State

Before the

Subcommittee on Asia and the Pacific
Of the House Committee on Foreign Affairs
July 30, 2014

U.S. Policy towards North Korea

Chairman Chabot, Representative Bera, and Members of the Committee, thank you for inviting my colleague Ambassador Robert King and me to testify today on U.S. policy toward the Democratic People's Republic of Korea (DPRK).

The DPRK government continues to make choices contrary to the interests of its people, its neighbors, and the world community. It flagrantly violates its obligations through its continued pursuit of nuclear weapons and ballistic missiles, posing a growing threat to the United States, our friends and allies in the region, and the global nonproliferation regime. It devotes scarce resources to its illicit weapons programs to its massive standing army, and to elaborate vanity projects for a privileged elite – all while the vast majority of North Korea's nearly 25 million people continue to suffer. More troubling, a UN Commission of Inquiry has concluded that in many instances, the violations it found the DPRK regime to have committed over decades constitute crimes against humanity. And in the last year, the DPRK has repeatedly threatened the United States, and its neighbors, the Republic of Korea and Japan. It is increasingly a global outlier in every sense.

We have no illusions about the nature of the regime, nor its intentions. We have refused to respond to DPRK provocations with concessions. North Korean has obtained no benefits from its bad behavior. Instead, we have tightened sanctions and consistently underscored to the DPRK that neither its occasional and tentative "charm" offensives nor its more frequent periods of aggressive behavior will lead us or the international community to accept a nuclear-armed North Korea. As we seek the negotiated complete, verifiable, and irreversible denuclearization of North Korea, we know we must keep pressure on Pyongyang or it will not give up the weapons it claims it needs. That is why our policy mix includes sanctions and traditional deterrence measures. In short, ours is a comprehensive approach that seeks to denuclearize North Korea through diplomacy while ensuring deterrence of the North Korean threat.

Diplomacy

We seek a solution to the North Korea nuclear challenge through peaceful, persistent, multilateral diplomacy. The United States has offered — and continues to offer — Pyongyang an improved bilateral relationship provided it takes action to demonstrate a willingness to fulfill its denuclearization commitments and address other important concerns which are also, we believe, shared by the international community. We have consistently signaled to the DPRK that the door for meaningful engagement is open while applying unilateral and multilateral pressure to steer it toward that door. Our policy has followed this dual-track approach: we are open to engagement when possible, but will continue to apply pressure as needed. Both elements are critical to sharpening Pyongyang's choices, demonstrating to the international community the seriousness of our commitment to a negotiated settlement of this issue, and building multilateral support for the various pressure and deterrence actions we take.

Regrettably, the DPRK has consistently rebuffed offers for authentic and credible negotiations and instead responded with a series of provocations that have drawn widespread international condemnation and increased its isolation. In just the past few weeks alone, the DPRK has conducted seven Scud-class ballistic missiles launches in direct violation of multiple UN Security Council resolutions. These followed short- and medium-range ballistic missile launches earlier this spring, which Pyongyang punctuated on March 30 with threats to conduct additional longer-range launches and possibly a "new type" of nuclear test.

The DPRK says it is ready for "talks without preconditions." No codebook is needed to decipher North Korea's intention: seek open-ended discussion that diverts attention away from its nuclear program and to avoid committing to denuclearization. Pyongyang has been explicit on this point: it seeks acceptance as a nuclear weapons state. It wants to use Six-Party talks, as it has in the past, as cover to continue its clandestine weapons development. We are not interested in Six-Party talks that do not focus directly on steps to implement, as a first and primary order of business, North Korea's September 2005 promise to denuclearize.

As a tactical matter, Pyongyang is asserting that the annual ROK-U.S. Ulchi-Freedom Guardian military exercises, which in 2014 will include representatives of ten United Nations' sending states, are a *casus belli*. It seeks to portray these routine, defensive, and transparent drills, which have helped ensure peace and stability on the Korean Peninsula for some 40 years, as a pretext for its provocative behavior and its weapons programs. Meanwhile, North Korea maintains — and frequently exercises — its own million-plus standing military, the largest per capita armed force in the world.

Six Party Diplomacy

The Six-Party Talks have regrettably been dormant since the DPRK walked out and declared the process "dead" in 2008. North Korea's 2009 Taepo Dong-2 launch and nuclear test then undermined the modest progress that had been made pursuant to the September 2005 Joint Statement of the Six-Party Talks. Since then, robust diplomatic interaction with the other four parties strengthened five-party unity on the end goal of the verifiable denuclearization of the Korean Peninsula. As a result, Pyongyang hears a uniform and clear message from all five parties, strongly echoed by the international community, that it will not be accepted as a nuclear power, that it must live up to its denuclearization obligations, and that authentic and credible negotiations must be marked by concrete denuclearization steps.

On this point it is important to be clear. None of the Five Parties insists North Korea denuclearize before returning to the negotiating table. But we have underscored we need to see an early and demonstrable commitment by the DPRK to denuclearize. This means the onus is on North Korea to take meaningful actions toward denuclearization and refrain from provocations.

Despite the DPRK's recidivism over the last half-decade, we remain committed to authentic and credible negotiations to implement the September 2005 Joint Statement of the Six-Party Talks and to bring North Korea into compliance with its international obligations through irreversible steps leading to denuclearization. But we will not engage in talks for the sake of talks and we will not compensate North Korea for the temporary absence of bad behavior. A resumption of Six-Party Talks makes sense if, and only if, there is plausible reason to believe that North Korea is prepared to negotiate seriously. North Korea knows this, but we have not yet seen signs that Pyongyang is prepared to meet its commitments and obligations to achieve the core goal of the September 2005 Joint Statement: the verifiable denuclearization of the Korean Peninsula in a peaceful manner.

Inter-Korean Relations

The Republic of Korea is firmly at the center of our diplomatic efforts. There is no daylight between Washington and Seoul on the issue of what we expect from North Korea. As President Obama emphasized during his public remarks in Seoul in April, the United States supports President Park's vision and desire for peaceful, progressive unification, as outlined in her March speech in Dresden, Germany. We hope to see Pyongyang take up President Park on her offer of an improved inter-Korean relationship. The DPRK — and the region — only stand to gain from embracing her principled vision.

The Role of China

Although we believe that there is more China can do in terms of bringing necessary pressure to bear on North Korea so that it concludes it has no choice but to denuclearize, Beijing has done a great deal. As North Korea's last remaining patron, the PRC has a critical, indeed unique, role to play in addressing the North Korean nuclear challenge.

That is why North Korea remains at the top of our bilateral agenda with China, and why it figured prominently in Secretary Kerry's discussions in Beijing in early July at the U.S.-China Strategic and Economic Dialogue. We welcome the steps the PRC has taken to signal its opposition to the DPRK's nuclear weapons program, including through its stated commitment to fully implement UN Security Council sanctions concerning North Korea. China voted in favor of two new rounds of UNSC sanctions and in September last year published a 900-item control list banning the export of many dual-use items to North Korea.

The United States and China share an interest in the peaceful denuclearization of North Korea. Beijing agrees with us on what North Korea needs to do – we have had the "what" of denuclearization nailed down since we negotiated the September 2005 Joint Statement. We are therefore now focused on coming to agreement on the "how" and the "when" of denuclearization. Can China do more to exercise its unique levers of influence over Pyongyang? Of course. And we remain in close touch with Beijing about ways we can work together to bring the DPRK to the realization that it has no other viable choice but to denuclearize.

Sanctions

We have no misconceptions about North Korea's willingness to give up its arsenal voluntarily. All of North Korea's actions over the past few years, from its nuclear tests to the amendment of its constitution to declare itself a nuclear state, signal that it has no interest in denuclearizing. We take this threat seriously, and remain ironclad in our commitment to the defense of our allies, the Republic of Korea and Japan. Together with our allies and partners, we are working to shift Pyongyang's calculus from believing that a nuclear program is necessary for regime survival to understanding that such a program is incompatible with its national interests.

To do that, we continue to use the multilateral and other tools at our disposal to increase the cost of North Korea's illicit activities, to reduce resources earned through weapons exports that are subsequently reinvested in the WMD program, and to sharpen Pyongyang's choices. Over the past two years, we have substantially upped the cost of these activities — particularly its proliferation and weapons sales abroad — by tightening the web of sanctions around the DPRK. We continue to work with a range of partners across the international community to improve implementation of UN Security Council sanctions, particularly those that target the illicit activities of the North's diplomatic personnel and cash couriers, its banking relationships, and its procurement of dual-use items for its WMD and missile programs.

Full and transparent implementation of these resolutions by all UN member states, including China, is critical. We are working closely with the UN Security Council's DPRK sanctions committee and its Panel of Experts, like-minded partners, and others around the globe to harmonize our sanctions programs and to ensure the full and transparent implementation of UNSCRs 1718, 1874, 2087, and 2094, which remain the heart of the multilateral sanctions regime. As a result, we have seen greater actions taken by Member States to prevent illicit North Korea trade in arms, WMD-related material and luxury goods, most notably with the seizure by Panama of a substantial amount of military gear on the North Korean ship Chong Chon Gang. The Panel's annual report documented in further detail the numerous actions that States have taken to enforce UN sanctions and prevent further DPRK proliferation. It is clear that UN sanctions are having an effect and are diminishing North Korea's ability to profit from its illicit activities.

The United States has expanded outreach to countries that have diplomatic or trade relations with North Korea to press them not to engage in military, WMD or other illicit activities banned by UN resolutions and U.S sanctions. Burma's announcement that it would end its military relationship with North Korea and comply with the UN resolutions is the best example of these efforts, which will continue. We have also designated a number of key proliferators — and the banks and other front companies that support them — pursuant to our domestic sanctions authorities. The United States will continue to take steps to strengthen and bolster the existing sanctions regime, both through work in the UN context and through our own national measures.

Deterrence

The U.S.-ROK alliance, having celebrated its 60th anniversary, is stronger than ever. From our day-to-day combined efforts to maintain peace and stability on the Peninsula, though our Combined Forces Command, to the counter-provocation and counter-missile planning our Department of Defense and Joint Staff colleagues engage in with their South Korean counterparts, we send a strong deterrence signal to North Korea that the security it is seeking is not to be found in nuclear weapons.

Our growing U.S.-ROK-Japan trilateral security cooperation also sends a powerful message of deterrence to Pyongyang, as seen most recently in our trilateral Search and Rescue Exercises, our July 1 Chiefs of Defense meeting between Chairman Dempsey and his counterparts in Seoul and Tokyo, the June 1 trilateral defense ministerial led by Secretary Hagel at the Shangri La dialogue, and my own periodic discussions with my able Korean and Japan counterparts. Other measures we have taken in the region to strengthen bilateral and trilateral missile defense cooperation are also inextricably tied to our larger diplomatic strategy of building and maintaining a strong diplomatic consensus opposed to a nuclear North Korea.

Human Rights

While denuclearization remains an essential focus of U.S. policy, so too, is the welfare of North Korea's nearly 25 million people, the vast majority of whom bear the brunt of their government's decision to perpetuate an unsustainable, self-impoverishing, military-first policy. As the UN Commission of Inquiry concluded in its impressive and sobering final report published this February, systematic, widespread, and gross human rights violations have been and are being committed by the DPRK, its institutions, and its officials.

I defer to my colleague, Special Envoy for North Korean Human Rights Issues Robert King, to brief you on our policy on North Korean human rights. Ambassador King's energetic and inspired efforts for over three years have demonstrated that the human rights issue remains a top priority and constant focus of the United States. He — and we — will continue to make clear to Pyongyang and the rest of the international community that U.S.-DPRK relations cannot fundamentally improve without progress on the human rights issue.

The U.S. government is deeply concerned about the well-being of the people of North Korea. We commend the non-governmental organizations and their staffs of skilled, tough-minded, and principled men and women who work with ordinary North Koreans at the grass-roots level to improve conditions for those who are not members of the elite, residing in relative comfort on Pyongyang. These men and women work tirelessly to feed, care for, and otherwise help sustain the ninety percent of North Koreans left to their own devices by the regime.

We believe those responsible for the human rights violations taking place in the DPRK must be held accountable for their ill treatment of their fellow citizens. We applaud the decision of the Republic of Korea to host the field office of the UN's Office of the High Commissioner for Human Rights to begin this work.

The Importance of Protecting American Citizens

The State Department makes clear in its DPRK travel warning that foreign visitors may be arrested, detained, or expelled for activities that would not be considered criminal outside North Korea. The list of serious transgressions is long. It includes involvement in religious or political activities unsanctioned by the DPRK regime, unauthorized travel, and unauthorized interaction with the local population. Given the serious risks involved, we strongly recommend against all travel by U.S. citizens to North Korea.

Despite the risks, a number of tour operators — mainly run out of Beijing by Westerners — organize highly-regimented trips to North Korea, principally to Pyongyang. Let me make this clear: tour operators cannot protect our citizens. We ask U.S. citizens contemplating travel to North Korea to understand the consequences of their decision.

Three U.S. citizens are, today, being held by the DPRK regime. We have no higher priority than the health and well-being of American citizens. We are doing all we can to seek their release so they may reunite with their families. Their continued detention also constitutes a serious impediment to improved U.S.-DPRK relations; it frankly renders disingenuous Pyongyang's assertion it wants a better relationship with the Unites States. Our thoughts are with our fellow citizens, and we will continue to advocate for their freedom — day in and day out — until we succeed. We remain grateful for Congress' steadfast support in these efforts.

Conclusion

Ultimately, Mr. Chairman, our policy aims to bring the DPRK to the realization that it must take the steps necessary to end its isolation, respect the human rights of its own people, honor its past commitments, and comply with its international obligations. Each outrageous act North Korea commits, discredits the DPRK's self-serving assertion that it is driven to act belligerently by others' hostility. It is increasingly clear that North Korea is developing nuclear weapons and intercontinental ballistic missiles to prolong the Kim regime and obtain material and political benefits from the international community. By creating a strategic challenge to the United States, the DPRK hopes to strengthen its narrative that the U.S. is responsible for North Korea's bad behavior and uniquely on the hook to mitigate it. It is not. North Korea is responsible for North Korean actions, and resolving the DPRK nuclear problem is a multilateral task, just as the DPRK's original aggression against the South was met with a strong response from the United Nations. Standing up to North Korea requires a sustained and concerted effort by all of the countries in the Six-Party process, and indeed the entire international community.

The DPRK leadership in Pyongyang faces ever-sharper choices. North Korea will not achieve security, economic prosperity, and integration into the international community while pursuing nuclear weapons, threatening its neighbors, trampling on international norms, abusing its own people, and refusing to fulfill its longstanding obligations and commitments.

Thank you again for the opportunity to appear before you today. I am happy to answer any questions you may have.

Mr. CHABOT. Thank you very much, Ambassador Davies. And we will now turn to Ambassador King. You are recognized for 5 minutes.

STATEMENT OF THE HONORABLE ROBERT KING, SPECIAL ENVOY FOR NORTH KOREAN HUMAN RIGHTS, OFFICE OF THE SPECIAL ENVOY FOR HUMAN RIGHTS IN NORTH KOREA, U.S. DEPARTMENT OF STATE

Mr. KING. Thank you very much, Mr. Chairman, Congressman Bera, members of the committee. Thank you for this invitation to testify with Ambassador Davies on U.S. policy on North Korea. I will focus on human rights aspects of our policy on which there has been broad bipartisan cooperation.

I want to thank you, Mr. Chairman, and committee members, for your interest in the North Korean human rights issues for the hearings that you have held, for the meetings that you have held both here and in Seoul and Tokyo with victims and their families.

North Korea remains a totalitarian state which seeks to dominate all aspects of its citizens' lives including denial of basic freedoms and human rights. Reports portray a vast network of political prison camps where individuals are subjected to forced labor under horrific conditions and the government commits human rights violations that include extrajudicial killing, enslavement, torture, prolonged arbitrary detention, abduction of foreign citizens as well as rape, forced abortion and other sexual violence.

This past year, we have made significant progress on our efforts to increase international pressure on the North, to improve its human rights. In March of last year, the U.N. Human Rights Council established a landmark Commission of Inquiry to examine grave, widespread, and systematic violation of human rights in North Korea. Refugees from North Korea gave the Commission first-hand accounts of abuse and violence and leading international experts described the government policies that repress their people. Public hearings were held in Seoul, Tokyo, London, and here in Washington, DC, video and written transcripts of those hearings are available on the U.N. Web site.

The Commission's final report was one of the strongest and finest reports that the U.N. has produced. The Commission concluded that the gross violations of human rights have been and continue to be committed by the North Korean Government and its officials. And in many cases, those violations meet the high standard, the high threshold required for proof of crimes against humanity and international law.

The Commission formally presented its final report of the Human Rights Council in March of this year. After hearing from the Commission, the Council overwhelmingly approved a resolution calling for accountability for those responsible for the abuses and for the creation of a field office under the High Commissioner for Human Rights to preserve and document evidence of these human rights abuses. South Korea has agreed to host this office.

Building on this momentum in April, the United States with Australia and France convened the first ever U.N. Security Council discussion of human rights in North Korea. The Commission presented its report. Two North Korean refugees spoke of their personal experiences. Eleven of the 13 Security Council members who attended that meeting expressed support for the report and called for accountability for the crimes that it outlined.

As I participated in the various U.N. meetings this past year, two things have struck me. First, it is clear that the North is feeling the growing international pressure. The mounting condemnation of its human rights record has struck a chord in Pyongyang. Second, with a growing number of countries critical of North Korean human rights, the only countries who defend the North are the world's worst human rights violators: Belarus, Cuba, Iran, Syria, Zimbabwe.

Mr. Chairman, another key human rights matter that I want to raise is our effort to increase access to information by the North Korean people. That country is one of the most closed societies on this planet. Internet access is reserved for a tiny, tiny elite. It is illegal to own a radio or television set that can be tuned to any channel other than the official government media. Anyone caught listening to foreign radio or television will be sent to a reeducation camp.

Despite these consequences of listening to foreign media, 35 percent of North Korean refugees and travelers listen to foreign radio broadcasts in North Korea. Foreign DVDs are now being seen by even larger numbers. Eighty-five percent of those interviewed have seen foreign, primarily South Korean media. Some 2 million cell phones for North Koreans to communicate with each other, although only domestic calls are permitted and phone use is carefully monitored.

Because of the closed nature of North Korea, our international media efforts are among the most effective we have of breaking the government's information monopoly. Thank you for continuing congressional support, for the Broadcasting Board of Governors and the media that it supports including Radio Free Asia and the Voice of America.

Finally, Mr. Chairman, I want to reiterate one point that Ambassador Davies has made. We have no greater priority than the welfare and safety of U.S. citizens abroad. We continue actively to seek the release on humanitarian grounds of Kenneth Bae, Matthew Miller, and Jeffrey Fowle, so that they may be reunited with their families.

Just as important as it is that North Korea address the issues that Ambassador Davies has talked about in terms of security and nuclear issues, it also must address its egregious human rights violations. The choice is clear. If North Korea does not take this action, it will continue to face greater isolation, condemnation, and increasing pressure from the international community.

Thank you, Mr. Chairman.

[The prepared statement of Mr. King follows:]

Testimony of Ambassador Robert King
Special Envoy for North Korean Human Rights Issues
U.S. Department of State

Before the

Subcommittee on Asia and the Pacific
Of the House Committee on Foreign Affairs
July 30, 2014

U.S. Policy on North Korean Human Rights

Chairman Chabot, Congressman Bera, and Members of the Committee, thank you for inviting me to testify today on U.S. human rights policy in the Democratic People's Republic of Korea (DPRK). This is an issue on which we believe there is broad bipartisan agreement, and both Congress and the Administration are united in our effort to press North Korea to improve its truly deplorable human rights situation.

Today, the DPRK remains a totalitarian state, which seeks to dominate all aspects of its citizens' lives, including denial of the freedoms of expression, peaceful assembly, association, religion, and movement, as well as worker rights. Reports continue to portray a vast network of political prison camps where individuals are subject to forced labor under horrific conditions and the government commits human rights violations including extrajudicial killing, enslavement, torture, prolonged arbitrary detention, and rape, forced abortions, and other sexual violence.

Mr. Chairman, this past year, we made significant progress in our effort to increase international pressure on the DPRK to improve its human rights record. The decision of the United Nations Human Rights Council (HRC) in March 2013 to create a Commission of Inquiry (COI) to examine "grave, widespread, and systematic violations of human rights" in the DPRK was a landmark event. This resolution, which the United States co-sponsored, reflects the international community's deepened concern about the deplorable human rights situation in the DPRK.

The independent Commission of Inquiry was chaired by Mr. Michael Kirby, former Justice of the High Court of Australia, and included Mr. Marzuki Darusman, the UN Special Rapporteur on the Human Rights Situation in the DPRK and former Attorney General of the Republic of Indonesia, and Ms. Sonia Biserko, president of the Helsinki Committee for Human Rights in Serbia and a prominent human rights activist.

The Commission held a series of public hearings in Seoul, Tokyo, London, and Washington, where it heard from North Korean refugees sharing first-hand accounts of abuse and violence they suffered, and their horrific experiences leaving their homeland. The Commission also heard from leading international experts, who described deliberate denial of access to food, gender-based violence, and numerous other human rights violations in the prison camps. The full proceedings of these hearings have since been made available on the UN web site in video and in written transcript.

At the completion of its investigation, the Commission issued a final report on February 17 of this year that concluded that systematic, widespread, and gross human rights violations have been and are being committed by the DPRK, its institutions, and its officials. The report further concluded that in many cases, these human rights violations by the DPRK government and its officials may "meet the high threshold required for proof of crimes against humanity in international law." The Commission's comprehensive 400-page report is the most detailed and devastating exposé of DPRK human rights to date, and it laid bare a brutal reality that is difficult, if not impossible, to imagine.

The Commission formally presented its final report to the UN Human Rights Council in Geneva in March of this year. After hearing from the Commission, the UN Human Rights Council—by an overwhelming vote approved a strongly-worded resolution praising the report and calling for accountability for those responsible for human rights violations. This resolution made clear that the international community has identified the DPRK as one of the worst human rights violators in the world.

This resolution—among many other things—called for the creation of a field office, or a "field-based structure," under the Office of the High Commissioner for Human Rights (OHCHR) to preserve and document evidence of atrocities committed in the DPRK and to support the future work of the Special Rapporteur on DPRK human rights issues.

At the request of the High Commissioner's office, South Korea has agreed to host this field office. We welcomed the decision to host this office, which will play an important role in maintaining visibility and encouraging action on the human rights situation in the DPRK.

Building on the momentum created by the UN Commission of Inquiry's report, the United States joined Australia and France in convening the UN Security Council's first-ever discussion of the human rights situation in North Korea. At this session on April 17, the Commission presented its report, and two North Korean refugees, Mr. Shin Dong Hyuk and Ms. Hyeonseo Lee spoke of their personal experiences in the DPRK before they escaped. Thirteen of the 15 members of the Security Council attended that discussion.

Council members expressed grave concern about the horrific human rights violations and crimes against humanity outlined in the Commission of Inquiry report and urged the DPRK to comply with the report's recommendations and to engage with United Nations human rights agencies. Council members emphasized the importance of accountability for human rights violations, and many expressed support for Council consideration of the Commission of Inquiry's recommendation of referral of the situation in North Korea to the International Criminal Court (ICC). They expressed support for the UN Human Rights Council's decision to extend the mandate of the Special Rapporteur on human rights in the DPRK and to establish a field-based office to strengthen monitoring and documentation of human rights abuses to ensure accountability.

In May, the United States participated in the UN Human Rights Council's Universal Periodic Review (UPR) of North Korea. The UPR is a mechanism to assess each country's human rights record, and puts *all* UN member-countries on the agenda of the Council for review. The UPR process provides the international community with another tool to discuss the situation in the DPRK, as well as provide recommendations to address it.

Most recently, on June 18, the Special Rapporteur on DPRK human rights, Mr. Marzuki Darusman, gave his report on the human rights situation to the UN Human Rights Council.

As I participated in these UN sessions, two things struck me. First, it is clear that the DPRK is feeling growing international pressure. The mounting criticism of its human rights record has clearly struck a chord in Pyongyang, which responded by condemning the Commission's report and issuing its own reports on human rights in the United States and the Republic of Korea.

Second, with a growing number of countries standing up for North Korean human rights, the DPRK has very few supporters left. At the UN Human Rights Council session in June, only a handful of countries were supportive of the DPRK—most protested the singling out of one country and did not comment on the substance of the human rights violations. The countries who defended the DPRK were among the world's worst human rights violators—Belarus, Cuba, Iran, Syria, and Zimbabwe.

China's statement at the June session was especially noteworthy. China objected to country-specific reports in general, but mainly defended itself against the criticism in both the Commission's and the Special Rapporteur's report against its refoulement of refugees from the DPRK who were attempting to escape through Chinese territory. The Chinese did not defend the DPRK's human rights record.

As I look back over what has taken place already this year to focus attention on the human rights record of North Korea, I am reminded of Commission of Inquiry Chair Michael Kirby's statement when he presented the Commission's report. With the body of evidence of the North Korean human rights situation, he said, no one can now say "We did not know."

Mr. Chairman, I would like to say a few words about another critical issue related to North Korean human rights: our efforts to increase North Koreans' access to information. When the Commission of Inquiry presented its report to the UN Human Rights Council, it also released a 20-minute documentary, highlighting testimony of North Korean defectors. Because North Korea is one of the most closed societies on this planet—where internet access is reserved for a very tiny elite—ordinary North Koreans had no way to see the documentary, let alone any independent news about the abuses taking place inside their own country today.

While this information blockade makes it nearly impossible for North Koreans to read the Commission's report or watch the video, we have recently seen modest indications that information from outside is becoming more available in North Korea.

It is still illegal to own a tunable radio that permits anything other than state-controlled information channels. However, the latest Broadcasting Board of Governors (BBG) study, a survey of 350 North Korean refugees and travelers who were interviewed outside of North Korea, found that:

- As many as 35 percent of them had listened to foreign radio broadcasts while inside North Korea.
- Foreign DVDs are now being seen by even larger numbers—approximately 85 percent of those interviewed had seen foreign (South Korean) DVDs in North Korea.
- Additionally, some two million cell phones now permit North Koreans to at least communicate with each other on a domestic network, according to open source reports.

Given the closed nature of North Korean society, international media are among the most effective means of sharing information about the outside world with residents of the country. Our government is a strong supporter of getting broadcasting of independent information about the outside world into North Korea. Thank you for continuing Congressional support for Radio Free Asia (RFA) and Voice of America (VOA). These efforts are important in breaking down the information barrier that the DPRK government has imposed on its own people.

Together with our partners in the international community, we must make clear to the DPRK that its egregious human rights violations prevent economic progress and weaken the regime. The United States has long made clear that we are open to improved relations with North Korea if it is willing to take concrete actions to live up to its international obligations and commitments.

Mr. Chairman, I would like to emphasize here that one of the highest priorities for the United States is the welfare and safety of American citizens abroad. The United States remains deeply concerned about the three U.S. citizens currently held by the DPRK. We have repeatedly requested that the DPRK grant them amnesty and release them so they may return to their families, and we will continue to do everything we can to secure their release.

The world will not, and cannot, close its eyes to what is happening in North Korea. Ultimately, we will judge the North not by its words, but by its actions. It needs to refrain from actions that threaten the peace and stability of the Korean Peninsula and comply with its international obligations under UN Security Council resolutions to abandon all nuclear weapons and nuclear programs, among other things.

We have consistently told the DPRK that while the United States remains open to meaningful engagement, North Korea must take concrete steps to address the core concerns of the international community, from the DPRK's nuclear program to its human rights violations.

Just as importantly, North Korea will also have to address its egregious human rights record. North Korea's choice is clear. Investment in its people, respect for human rights, and concrete steps toward denuclearization can lead to a path of peace, prosperity, and improved relations with the international community, including the United States. Absent these measures, North Korea will only continue to face greater and greater isolation—as well as pressure from the international community.

Mr. CHABOT. Thank you very much, Mr. Ambassador. Members will now have 5 minutes to ask questions and I will begin with myself.

Ambassador Davies, on July 20th, Secretary Kerry was quoted as saying that North Korea has been quieter. I wouldn't describe the historic number of missiles and rocket and artillery launches this year—so far nearly 100—as quiet. I also don't believe that solely because North Korea hasn't staged another nuclear test this year that we would necessarily call Pyongyang's behavior quiet. Can you perhaps clarify why Secretary Kerry is describing North Korea as such and tell us how you can justify that classification?

Mr. DAVIES. Mr. Chairman, the Secretary said a lot of things. That was one thing he said and I think that to kind of place it back in context, the Secretary was referring to the fact that we are now some time on from the last major strategic provocation by North Korea. It has been a while since they have either launched a three stage intercontinental ballistic missile or tested a nuclear device.

Mr. CHABOT. Do you think he would want to rephrase that perhaps differently or would you?

Mr. DAVIES. I think in context it is easy to understand what the Secretary was saying which is that the cooperation, the collaboration, the diplomacy that we have been conducted with South Korea, China, and other partners in the process has gotten the message through to Pyongyang that when it acts strategically, when it tests a nuclear device and it is the only country on earth to have done it in this century, when it launches a three stage intercontinental ballistic missile that the world will react, it will react strongly and unanimously. So I think that is what the Secretary is referring to.

It is absolutely the case and the Secretary has also spoken to this as have other senior officials, that North Korea's recent behavior is unacceptable. The fact that it continues time after time to launch these ballistic missiles, violates U.N. Security Council resolutions, that cannot be countenanced——

Mr. CHABOT. I would certainly agree with you and the administration that it is unacceptable. I certainly wouldn't have called it quieter, but that is okay.

I am going to turn to Ambassador King if I can at this time. Ambassador, you have done a commendable job representing the North Korea human rights portfolio. I also recognize the difficulties you face since the administration doesn't make the human rights issue, in my view, enough of a top priority. I think at best it is a second-tier issue behind nuclear proliferation, even if it is given sometimes lip service by calling it a top priority and constant focus. As such, I am disappointed that following the release of the U.N. Commission of Inquiry Report—in my view—little has been done. No human rights sanctions, no executive orders, and no move for a vote in the Security Council. Ambassador King, can you tell us what is being done at this time to hold North Korea accountable for the mass atrocities described in that report? I mean, it was a horrific thing to read, and there has been so little movement since the report's release. Also, are you aware that there are three Americans currently detained in Pyongyang? I am deeply concerned particularly about their well-being and safety and one of those individuals, Jeffrey Fowle, he is from right outside my district in Ohio. I am told he is being brought to trial, accused of carrying out hostile acts against the country. Can you provide us with an update about this situation and where in the process the administration is to get these individuals released out of North Korea? And I certainly understand in a forum like this, you have to be careful because we don't want to jeopardize their situation or put them in any more jeopardy than they already are. So I understand that, but to the degree that we can, in a forum like this, I would appreciate some comment.

Mr. KING. Thank you very much for the question, Mr. Chairman. With regard to the attention that we give to North Korea human rights, I believe it was Lyndon Johnson that said, "You have got to be able to walk and chew gum at the same time." I think that is what we are trying to do in terms of pushing on both the nuclear issue, but also pushing on the human rights issue. And I think as we have talked earlier, there is a lot that has been done this year with the release of the report. We have been attempting to use the U.N. report to continue to put pressure on North Korea. In the U.N. Security Council, we have already had an informal meeting where we have had 13 of the 15 members attend, discuss the report and discuss its recommendations.

We are also in the process of looking toward activity in Geneva. We will continue our pressure in Geneva, the Human Rights Council on the human rights report. We are also going to have discussions in the General Assembly in October at which the Commission of Inquiry's report will be discussed. There will be a resolution that will be prepared and adopted in the General Assembly by the end of this year. We are very active in terms of looking at how we might further push this forward in terms of action with the Security Council.

With regard to sanctions, we are looking at sanctions. One of the issues that we need to do is try to do whatever we do in concert with other countries. Sanctions by the United States alone are very limited effectiveness. We have very little relationship with North Korea. We have very little trade. We have very little economic connection. And to the extent that we can work together with our allies and jointly adopt sanctions and look at actions that we can take together, I think the more effective those issues will be.

A brief quick comment. The three Americans who are being held in North Korea are of great concern to us. We have communicated with the North Koreans our concern. We have requested repeatedly that they be released on humanitarian grounds. This includes Mr. Fowle, as well as Kenneth Bae and Matthew Miller. We are hoping to be able to have some progress on that. We continue to press the North Koreans. We have continued to work through the Swedish Government which takes care of our interest with regard to American citizens there. I briefed your staff on this. I know you were aware of that. If there is anything that we can provide you directly, I would be happy to come up and talk with you about that.

Mr. CHABOT. Thank you for that. I would like to continue to follow up with you at the staff level on Mr. Fowle, in particular, but all of them. Thank you very much.

I now recognize the acting ranking member, the gentleman from California, Mr. Bera.

Mr. BERA. Thank you, Chairman Chabot. Ambassador Davies, in your opening testimony, I think you laid a framework that said any movement forward really starts with the framework that was laid out in the 2005 Six-Party Talks. That is a starting point for us to move forward.

Also, Ambassador King and Ambassador Davies, in describing North Korea, you described them as global pariah. We described the crimes against humanity, the human rights violations. And it is from this vantage point when you look at the Kim regime, it is a regime that is less focused on its people and more focused on itself. I empathize with the difficulty of these negotiations. We can continue to further isolate North Korea, but we have also seen when we do that isolation how the Kim regime responds in provocative manners. I think you accurately lay out that this is not a U.S.-North Korea negotiation. This is a U.S.-Japan-Korea-China-Russia negotiation in the framework of regional stability. And of those countries, we all have a vested interest in creating a stable region, but the key really in this case lies with an active engagement on China's behalf.

I guess, Ambassador Davies, I would like you to comment on the talks that we have had with China, how China is viewing the new North Korean regime, and comment on China's role in moving these conversations forward.

Mr. DAVIES. I would be happy to do that, sir. Thanks so much. China and North Korea are not at their best historical comment right now. China was very vocal and active beginning over 2 years ago when the new third generation of leadership took over in Pyongyang in signaling to the North Korean regime that they would not support North Korea taking provocative acts and North Korea went ahead and did it. So in a sense North Korea has not been a good partner of China's of late. And this has triggered, I think, a debate in China about the nature of its relationship with North Korea. The Chinese have begun to take acts that are somewhat remarkable in the historical scheme of things, publicly signaling and warning North Korea not to engage in strategic provocations, publishing this 900 item control list which is somewhat dramatic, cutting off banking relations with the Foreign Trade Bank of North Korea, also imposing strictures on some customs controls and so forth.

So our role in this is to work with the Chinese to try to figure out and this is the top down. The President has been very engaged in this from the Sunnylands Summit of last summer on forward and a series of meetings with Xi Jinping how can the United States and China in a bilateral diplomacy, but also working with our other partners and the five parties to convince North Korea that its future does not lie in pursuing these weapons of mass destruction. Its future lies in living up to the promises that it made in the middle of the last decade abandoning the weapons, coming back into the fold of the international community, behaving better as an international actor, and the Chinese have done these unprecedented things. We have said to China that we appreciate it very much. We said there is only one problem with the acts that China has taken and that is, of course, that they haven't yet worked to fundamentally change the calculus of Pyongyang. So this is a work in progress. But we have made progress. And we are going to keep at it.

I think the new leadership in Beijing understands they can't retain the status quo forever and this is a case where I think if we keep at it, in a multilateral endeavor, with the ROK at the core of our concerns and our diplomacy, China also quite central that we can ultimately make progress.

Mr. BERA. And if we look at this North Korean regime that is provocative and potentially unstabling in the region, as inter-trade and inter-dependence, increasing trade between Korea and China, Japan and China, ourselves and China, our economies are increasingly interconnected in trade and we all benefit from a stable region that allows trade to occur. There is a real—China has to recognize that an unstable region is not in China's interest and really creates some problems. So we do have to move forward in a regional conversation. We do have to move forward in partners. And I hope China is there increasing the pressure and isolating North Korea that they are on the wrong path. Thank you. I will yield back.

Mr. CHABOT. The gentleman's time has expired. Thank you very much. We will now recognize the gentleman from Pennsylvania, Mr. Perry, for 5 minutes.

Mr. PERRY. Thank you, Mr. Chairman. Gentlemen, thanks for being here. I was a little late, so I missed your testimony, but listened to some of the answers to the questions. It just gave me some new questions and some new things to think about.

Mr. Davies, you talked about we have made gains. And one of my questions is going to be this strategy of strategic patience and many would contend that it really hasn't done anything and my question would be what are the significant results of that?

Quite honestly, I feel like asking what are the significant or insignificant results from the context, maybe I should first ask this strategy of strategic patience what is the time frame of this? Are we looking at like 1,000 years? Or 100 years? Is this my lifetime? Because convincing North Korea's leadership that this isn't their pathway to the future, who are we kidding?

Does anybody in this room think that these people have the same mindset about their future that the people in here have? The leadership? Maybe peasants, maybe the under class, maybe the people cited in the Human Rights Council report have that view of some brighter future possibly and that it should change.

What would motivate the people at the top to change anything? I am really curious. Let me give you a question. What are the significant or insignificant results? How long is this strategy supposed to go and what makes you think that these folks would change their mindset whatsoever?

Mr. DAVIES. Well, a couple of things. Strategic patience is like a bumper sticker that gets stuck on a car and just doesn't get taken off even when the views of the driver change. I have been at this job 2½ years. I have never described our policy as strategic patience. So it predates me. It is inaccurate.

Secretary of State, when he was asked about it when he first came into office said no, that is not our policy. Our policy is strategic impatience with North Korea. We are going to continue to do everything we can not to sit down and have a coffee klatch with them and try to convince them of the logic of it, but to use pressure in particular, to point out to them that there is only one way forward. It is the peaceful diplomatic path forward. It is living up to their obligations, commitments, and promises that they made freely 11 years ago and it is going down this path of denuclearization.

So I think what they care about most in Pyongyang, this regime, is surviving. They want to preserve the status quo. They don't want anything to rock their boat. They are now—it is the world's only historical example of a dynastic communist system, father to son, now in the third generation. They want to keep that party obviously going on.

What we are doing, what we are seeking to do with China, South Korea, Japan, Russia and the rest of the international community is pump up the volume of a message to North Korea that that is the road to ruin for North Korea, that trying to pour scarce resources into the development of these expensive weapon systems while also trying to feed their people which they have not been able to do adequately for now almost a generation isn't going to work. So what they need to do is give up these weapons, begin to play by the rules, begin to live up to their own promises——

Mr. PERRY. Listen, I don't mean to just completely interrupt you and I am trying to listen. I have got a limited amount of time, but pumping up the volume on rhetoric, they are hoping to keep it going. And as far as the West or somebody in the West or our coalition partners telling them that it is not going to work from their perspective at the top, well, it has worked for three generations. We are not going to rock the boat. And with all due respect, folks, the Human Rights Council includes the likes of Cuba and the Democratic Republic of the Congo, and some of these bad actors that abuse their own citizenry and acting like that is going to be a vehicle to shake North Korea's leadership off its foundation.

I would like to have whatever you folks are drinking and eating every day because you have got a wonderful view of some rose-colored future. To me, we are the United States. Now listen, I am not trying to pose—this is a 20-year-old failure in my opinion or so it is not fair to impose all this upon you, but taking the same actions of the past, okay, it is not strategic—to me, it is strategic apathy or avoidance or something. I don't know what it is, but doing the same over and over again for the next 20, 30, 40 years and expecting a different outcome, if I were here in 40 years, we are going to be having the same conversation. You can go ahead and comment, but I am frustrated.

Mr. DAVIES. Look, again, we are not just talking about diplomatic messaging and sending them nice letters. We are talking about cutting off the inputs to their weapons programs through sanctions, through interdiction. And there have been successes there. When Panama rolled up the largest shipment of North Korean conventional weapons in July of last year on a Korean freighter trying to go through the Panama Canal, that was an indicator that the rest of the world gets the message, when 80 countries condemned North Korea's decision to test a nuclear device beginning of last year and took action to join with the sanctions regime internationally to impose costs on North Korea, that is what we are talking about here.

No, we are not talking about some kind of a hortatory attempt to convince them through a high school debating society. We are talking about taking actions that reduce their running room, that cut off their resources, that prevent them from selling the weapons systems that they need to sell in order to get the inputs for their weapons programs.

But we are also talking about keeping a hand open to North Korea if they have this change of mind. That is the diplomacy part of it. I was engaged in negotiating with them at the beginning of 2012. We cut a very modest deal with them that could have given them a chance back to what they claim they want which is security guarantees and all the rest of it and they chose not to take it. Instead, they launched a rocket in honor of the 100th anniversary of his grandfather's birth. That was his choice to make. The result of it was near universal condemnation and action taken by nation states.

It is a little bit like watching paint dry. I understand that. The Cold War took three generations. Sometimes, these problems are so pernicious that they simply take the patient application of increasing amounts of pressure accompanied by diplomacy in order to get these actors to realize that they are going down a path that leads them nowhere. And so that is our strategy. If there is an alternative, we are all ears.

Mr. CHABOT. The gentleman's time has expired. And I would like to associate myself with the frustrations of the gentleman from Pennsylvania. I think they are well said.

The gentleman from Virginia is recognized for 5 minutes.

Mr. CONNOLLY. Well, if we are associating ourselves with frustration, I am frustrated, too, and I am sure you are and I am sure everyone in the audience is. I am not quite sure what the relevance of our frustration is to try to fashion an efficacious public policy that creates change. And I would like to explore that with both of our witnesses.

First of all, as you know or may know, we managed a bill the other day on the floor, Chairman Royce and myself, that passed unanimously adding to the sanctions regime on North Korea and I assume you both probably were aware of that and I welcome your reaction. I assume you support it and hopefully if it becomes law, we can use it as another tool in the kit bag.

Ambassador Davies?

Mr. DAVIES. For us, it is a bit of a third rail to be commenting on pending legislation, so I am going to steer clear of that with your permission. I think sanctions are a tool that is of value and I think we have demonstrated that through the actions we have taken both unilaterally and working with our partners around the world. We remain very open to further sanctions and options, when and if they make sense to deploy them, to use them. I am committed to finding a multilateral way forward. I wish there were a silver bullet we could fire to solve this problem.

Mr. CONNOLLY. Right.

Mr. DAVIES. Smarter people than me would have figured it out long ago.

Mr. CONNOLLY. Let us explore that just a little bit. Where do you think the pressure points are? I heard what you were saying about China which was quite intriguing, but in some ways if China has lost leverage over the regime of Pyongyang, well then where are the pressure points that the West can turn to or South Korea can turn to to try to rein in behavior or reward good behavior, punish bad behavior? I mean where are those leverage points?

Mr. DAVIES. Well, China hasn't lost leverage. They have just decided there are limits to the leverage that they are willing to exercise. So when it comes to food and fuel for North Korea, China is absolutely critical in that respect. So there is more that China could do. But we think it works much better if the world and in particular the neighbors of North Korea act together on this, supported by the rest of the international community.

The Achilles heel of North Korea is the fact that it doesn't have sufficient fossil fuels. It is unable to feed itself because it has broken its own economic system, hollowed it out over the years. And so in terms of ways to put pressure on them, these are some of the ways that we can use to do that.

Mr. CONNOLLY. And I appreciate that, but I was thinking about the normal kinds of leverage when you look at sanctions regimes, we are looking at it on Russia right now. Well, the ruble is exchanged. They have a stock market. They have external investment. They had trade flows, all of which can now be influenced in a way they were not as influenced when they were the Soviet Union. So they are feeling some heat.

We don't really have that kind of leverage with the North Korea regime, do we?

Mr. DAVIES. We have limited leverage because we have almost no trade with them.

Mr. CONNOLLY. Right.

Mr. DAVIES. That is correct.

Mr. CONNOLLY. And of course, they use their nuclear program as leverage over the West in terms of food supplies, emergency food supplies and the like.

Mr. DAVIES. That is correct.

Mr. CONNOLLY. Yes.

Mr. DAVIES. But I should say one of the biggest points of leverage we have is the strength of our alliance relationships and in particular with the Republic of Korea because it is their peninsula, but also with Japan and staying strong and solidarity building up our alliance and our ability to defend our friends and ourselves against North Korean threats is a huge part of what we have.

Mr. CONNOLLY. Let me just in the last minute I have got, explore China's relationship again. If I understood your testimony in a sense there has been a reassessment in China about the nature of the relationship with the regime in Pyongyang. Is that your testimony?

Mr. DAVIES. They are debating it, that is correct.

Mr. CONNOLLY. Okay, they are debating it. Do you believe that as part of that debate the new leadership in Beijing is—well, first of all, the economic ties to South Korea are far more important for Beijing, frankly, than North Korea, is that not true?

Mr. DAVIES. Many multiples.

Mr. CONNOLLY. Right. So given their exposure and the fact that they are stakeholders in the success of the capitalist Korea economy, are they, do you believe, more open to pressuring the North for say market reforms, similar to their own?

Mr. DAVIES. They have been trying to convince North Korea for years to engage in reform of their economy and the North Koreans have resisted that.

Mr. CONNOLLY. What leverage are the Chinese prepared to use to rein in belligerent behavior, try to achieve some of those market reforms, and are they prepared, do you believe, in some kind of timetable to move eventually toward an accommodation with the South, if not outright reunification with the South?

Mr. CHABOT. The gentleman's time has expired, but you can answer the question.

Mr. DAVIES. I think this is one of the fascinating conversations that has sort of occurred during the recent summit meeting between President Xi Jinping and Park Geun-hye of South Korea and it is fascinating that Beijing is voting with its feet, that now the President of China has met multiple times with his counterpart in South Korea, has yet to meet with, travel to North Korea. So things are beginning to change. I wish they were faster, but these are the changes we are observing.

Mr. CHABOT. The gentleman from North Carolina, Mr. Holding, is recognized for 5 minutes.

Mr. HOLDING. Thank you, Mr. Chairman. Mr. Davies, how has Rouhani's regime altered the North Korea-Iran relationship?

Mr. DAVIES. I am not sure I am qualified to describe what is happening between those two countries other than that we watch very closely any proliferation or signs of proliferation that might exist between North Korea and his regime.

Mr. HOLDING. Does the administration have any evidence or reason to suggest that North Korea and Iran have intentionally focused on different aspects of nuclear weapons capability to speed up the final results for both countries?

Mr. DAVIES. Well, sir, with great respect, you are starting to get me down deep into intelligence matters and these are the sorts of things we would be very happy to brief you on in a closed hearing, but again, it is a matter of serious concentration and strong study by the administration.

Mr. HOLDING. Given Iran and North Korea's cooperation in the past, do you think it is likely that North Korea would share any future nuclear test data with Iran?

Mr. DAVIES. You are calling for speculation on the part of the witness. I just don't know.

Mr. HOLDING. I don't think we are bound by the Federal rules of civil——

Mr. DAVIES. I am sorry. I am trying to be a little glib. But no, again, I think intelligence information——

Mr. HOLDING. The witness will answer the question.

Mr. CHABOT. Thank you, Your Honor. You may proceed.

Mr. DAVIES. Pardon me, would you like to restate that?

Mr. HOLDING. It is a concern of Iran and North Korea have cooperated in the past.

Mr. DAVIES. I think there is every incentive between them to co-operate in some aspect to this, that is correct.

Mr. HOLDING. And you don't think there is any—the Rouhani regime coming in hasn't changed any of that dynamic there that would lead to that—that has led to the cooperation in the past?

Mr. DAVIES. Not that I am aware of, but one would hope that there would be changes.

Mr. HOLDING. Your report suggests that North Korean energy needs have been met by Iran and that Iran's desire for armaments have been met by North Korea. Reports have suggested that cooperation. What do we know about trends in oil consumption by North Korea and if they are stockpiling Iranian oil?

Mr. DAVIES. I am not aware of the provision of Iranian oil to any great extent I have got to say to North Korea. I am just not aware of that.

Mr. HOLDING. Switching to Russia a little bit, how have increased tensions between Russia and the West affected Russia's relationship with North Korea?

Mr. DAVIES. Well, Russia's relationship with North Korea fundamentally changed in 1989, 1990 when the Soviet Union disappeared and the client relationship that existed disappeared. And so now they have a very, very small economic relationship quite frankly. They have a political relationship, but it is not nearly as important as that between Beijing and Pyongyang, between China and North Korea.

Mr. HOLDING. So you don't believe that the Russians have intensified or accelerated any weapons sales to North Korea in recent years?

Mr. DAVIES. I am not aware of anything significant in that regard, no, sir.

Mr. HOLDING. North Korea skirts international sanctions in a lot of different respects. One thing, I believe they are one of the largest suppliers of counterfeit cigarettes in the world, believe it or not, counterfeit currency as well. Any current administration actions to close these loopholes and more rigidly enforce the sanctions that you would like to expound on for 1 minute and 10 seconds?

Mr. DAVIES. Sure. From the standpoint on counterfeit goods, there was a day when that was a booming business. I think that that day has passed to some extent, that that is something that we watch very, very closely, but North Korea will obviously stop at nothing to try to gain resources to develop its weapons programs and that is why we concentrate so much energy on nonproliferation, not just unilaterally with our friends and allies and partners.

Mr. HOLDING. All right. Thank you, Mr. Chairman.

Mr. CHABOT. Thank you. The gentleman yields back. The gentleman from Georgia, Mr. Collins, is recognized for 5 minutes.

Mr. COLLINS. Thank you, Mr. Chairman. In listening to your testimony, I think it is rather interesting, again, with one of the key players, with basically the rogueness of North Korea and whether their relationship with Iran at least something studied a little bit more and I think using your words and I may have gotten this just a little bit wrong, but it was something to the effect of study and watching what is going on. That to me, and there is something in your written testimony that says ultimately, Mr. Chairman, our policy is to bring to realization that North Korea must take steps necessary to end its isolation, respect the human rights of its own people, honor its past commitments and national obligations.

In light of that, what we will call the desirous goal, many experts contend that the administration's strategy of strategic patience or basically watch and see, has not yet yielded any significant results, but rather has served only to benefit North Korea by offering it more time or affording it more time to pursue its own objectives. What is the administration's assessment of its strategy of engagement and strategic patience?

Mr. DAVIES. Our assessment is that we have made some progress, not nearly enough. We have got a lot further to go.

Mr. COLLINS. What would you say your greatest accomplishment is?

Mr. DAVIES. I think our greatest accomplishment is in achieving in just the last couple of years two United Nations Security Council resolutions with teeth that had attached with them resolutions. These were unanimously achieved. China voted for them. Russia voted for them. And Hezbollah, Hamas, Iran, this whole nexus of issues which I know is very important to you, we are doing more than just studying and watching this. Obviously, what we are doing is seeking to disrupt illicit shipments, enforce these sanctions. We are doing it with our partners. We know that they would naturally like to deal with each other, but we are doing everything we can to prevent that from developing.

Mr. COLLINS. I think in the end is what other things beyond two United Nations resolutions which may or may not have the teeth and the enforcement that some would like to see, beyond that, what is the next step? What is the next big accomplishment? What is the next thing to ensure basically what you said is your own goals, is to encourage North Korea to become a model citizen which under the current leadership I am not even sure it understands the definition of model citizenship. It is a discussion here to have. What would be the next process?

Mr. DAVIES. Well, we would settle for North Korea starting to do what it promised to do a long time ago and has tentatively started to do in the past which is to take steps in the direction of denuclearizing. In other words, freezing their nuclear programs, inviting the IAEA back in to inspect them, eventually leading to the dismantlement and elimination of the North Korean nuclear weapons program. That is the foundation of the six party process that we have been engaged in for many years and we have made a great deal of progress with particularly China, keeping the solidarity of Japan and the ROK with us.

There is no daylight between any of the three of the allies, in order to get North Korea moving down that path of denuclearization. They are far away from it. And therefore, we are in a pressure phase. And that is what we have concentrated a lot of energy on is putting pressure on North Korea so that it understands it only has one option and that is the peaceful diplomatic option of denuclearization.

Mr. COLLINS. And I understand there is some issue and I was discussing it with my very capable staff this discussion with Iran and going about that issue, but there seems to be at least somewhere along the line for North Korea, there is at least some ways around what has been "put in place for strategic containment and isolation" for them because at this point some of that is just not, in fact, if anything, there has been actual—I won't say regression, but there has definitely not been a lot of progress shown. They seem to be happily going about the fact that they are isolated and would like to get back, but they want to do so on their terms.

So I guess the concern and the good part about—and I appreciate the chairman having this discussion—is just simply the fact of working through others which is a good thing, working with others, but somewhere there is a gap in the system. Somewhere there seems to be again rogue nations, others who will have dealings with North Korea and not pursuing these assets and I think that is where maybe a situation which there is a much bigger stick along with a carrot that maybe can influence this and especially with our South Korean partners in this process as well.

Again, I think it is not an easy situation to answer and I appreciate your answers. Thank you.

Mr. DAVIES. Thank you.

Mr. CHABOT. Thank you. The gentleman yields back. We will go to a second round. I think there will just be two of us here, so we should be wrapped up within 10 minutes and I think we are going to have votes here shortly. I will begin with myself here.

Recently, Japan and North Korea have reengaged on the issue of Japanese nationals abducted by North Korean agents back in the '70s and the '80s, an issue that froze relations for the past number of years. In fact, I met with the Yokota family whose daughter, Megumi Yokota, was abducted by North Korean agents back in 1977 at the age of 13 and I have met with them a number of times over the years, as well as a number of the other families. It is truly a sad and outrageous story.

Pyongyang agreed to further investigate the fate of Japanese abductees in exchange for Tokyo's lifting some sanctions which they apparently agreed to do. And it is a pretty sad state of affairs when you can leverage kidnapped citizens for some relief in sanctions. My question is, what do you think will be the likely outcome of this agreement? What is North Korea's motivation for reopening the investigations? And how much advance notice did the administration have before Japan and North Korea reached their agreement? Do you have any concerns about these negotiations considering North Korea's long record of deception and deceit?

Mr. DAVIES. Well, we stand with Japan in terms of their desire which we completely understand to try to resolve this humanitarian catastrophe. I have met with the Yokotas a number of times myself. I was there with our new Ambassador, Ambassador Kennedy, when she first met with the Yokotas and the families of abductees, so we understand why not just the government, but the people of Japan want this resolved and we support them in their efforts to do this. The Japanese have kept us very closely informed as they have taken these steps, these limited steps, with North Korea. And we have indicated to Japan and we have said publicly that we are supportive of all of the efforts that Japan is undertaking as long as they are undertaken transparently. And obviously, what is very important for all of us and it is shared concern of the Japanese is that we have this paramount concern of the North Korean nuclear missile threat and the Japanese have been very explicit in indicating to us that they agree with that very much.

We will watch. We are supportive of it. And we will see where it heads. North Korea is now on the hook. They have got to conduct this investigation that they promised the Japanese that they would conduct and so we will be watching very closely to see what kinds of results the North Koreans come up with and whether or not it meets the tests that the Japanese are imposing on them.

Mr. CHABOT. Also, Ambassador Davies, in your prepared statement, you said that China is "North Korea's last remaining patron." Considering its budding relationship with Russia and illicit networks with countries in the Middle East, Iran especially, I wonder if that is completely accurate. And the recent economic trade deal between Russia and North Korea comes at a very opportune time for Pyongyang. It provides Pyongyang with an economic boost that it needs to counter the sanctions and also to counter balance the Chinese who have been putting some pressure on them but not nearly enough in the opinion of many of my colleagues and I. And for Russia, this deal undermines U.S. efforts to cut off North Korea's financial and economic well being while enhancing its own web of influence vis-à-vis the U.S. in, for example, the Ukrainian crisis. Can you tell us what sort of goods Russia is providing to North Korea, weapons, or oil, or gas, or food? And how is the Russian-North Korean relationship being considered as part of the administration's strategic calculus and efforts to effectively pressure North Korea since Russia is also trying to bolster ties with China. Is anything being done to counter this trilateral cooperation between these nations?

Mr. DAVIES. Well, Mr. Chairman, actually the Russia-North Korea relationship is very, very small in terms of trade. And some of the steps that Moscow announced were basically a recognition of the existing state of affairs. For instance, they announced some debt relief for North Korea. I don't think anybody in Moscow ever expected that they would get that debt repaid to begin with.

The trade is measured in a few hundreds of millions of dollars a year. They have been talking about some new projects that could be of interest, infrastructure projects. These are longer term undertakings and so far they are still a bit at the margins. So we stay in touch with the Russians. I go out to Moscow and try to talk to them about this problem. We have a shared interest in denuclearization and this is serious on the part of Russia. Russia is a stakeholder in the nonproliferation treaty. They don't want North Korea to develop nuclear weapons. I think they are serious about that. We may have tactical differences there that we are going to continue to work on. But right now, I think it is fair to say that the agreement, the level of agreement that we have on strategic issues with Russia outweighs some of these deals that they are talking about at the margins right now.

Mr. CHABOT. Thank you very much. My time has expired. The gentleman from California is recognized.

Mr. BERA. Thank you, Chairman. My staff has given me an article from The Hill, from yesterday's paper that says North Korea threatens nuclear strikes on the White House. I am not going to take that seriously, other than maybe they are watching some DVDs from Hollywood as well that are getting smuggled in. But I do take seriously that they continue to try to develop longer range missile technology and so forth and as they acquire and develop that technology, they really are a threat to not only our regional partners and allies, but Guam and some of our territories all the way to Hawaii that we do have to take very seriously. And that does create a sense of urgency in moving things forward.

My colleague from Virginia, Mr. Connolly, kind of underscored the challenge here. Sanctions with a regime that does not seem to care about what happens to its people are very difficult and all indications suggest that the Kim regime is not taking the interest of the North Korean people at stake here. So they are the ones that clearly are suffering. But we have a limited tool box here. So certainly as we ratchet up those sanctions just thinking through various scenarios, Chairman Chabot touched on your opening testimony, Ambassador Davies, where China is North Korea's last remaining patron. What would happen if China joined us in the sanctions, if we are just thinking through and really did cut North Korea off? How would North Korea respond?

Mr. DAVIES. Well, China has said that they support fully the United Nations sanctions And I talked about some of the signs that the Chinese are beginning to take really unprecedented action in that direction, the signal to North Korea that they will pay a price if they don't come around in particular on the nuclear issue.

This is why when we talk to the Chinese, we try to talk about how we can work in concert to bring pressure to bear on the North Koreans in a surgical way because we don't want to do anything to the people of North Korea, but we do want to affect the interests of the regime when it comes to obtaining these weapons. And we are going to keep at that because we think increasingly the core Chinese interests and stability on the Korean Peninsula and our core interests in security that these are converging concerns. And we are seeing signs for the first time in decades that the Chinese also recognize this, that their stability will be affected unless we can address proactively North Korea's pursuit of these weapons. And so that is where we are concentrating our energy and we are saying to the Chinese there is more you can do. We respect the fact that you are going to make decisions about how you do it, but we need to do more. And it is more effective if we can do it together with our partners.

Mr. BERA. What we need to do this in partnership is we are increasingly showing North Korea there really is only one path forward, that is de-escalation, denuclearization and becoming a more conventional nation.

Shifting to a different scenario, again, North Korea continues to posture with missiles toward the South Korean border and so forth. Again, not helpful. What would South Korea's response be at this juncture? I think South Korean has shown incredible restraints, given some of North Korea's provocation in recent years, if in fact, there was a misfire accidentally or intentionally that were to land in a South Korean city. Seoul is not that far away and what have the South Koreans indicated that their response would be at this juncture?

Mr. DAVIES. The South Koreans are increasingly resolved that should there be a provocation on the part of North Korea, that they will respond. This is, of course, due to the fact that in 2010 there were two deadly attacks by North Korea on South Korea, that resulted in some deaths of South Korean civilians. So this is what our alliance with South Korea is all about, ensuring that together we can present this united front on the peninsula to North Korea and they can understand that they can't repeat the aggression that they portrayed on the South in June 1950, that those days are gone and that the best path forward is, in fact, the vision that has been laid out by the President of South Korea who has talked about a path forward involving peaceful unification, people to people, infrastructure development and so forth and so far Pyongyang, North Korea, has rejected that.

Mr. BERA. And I would want to make sure that the people in South Korea know that, as one of our close allies in the region, we do stand with them in this and the right to defend themselves.

Mr. DAVIES. Absolutely.

Mr. BERA. And to make sure that those listening in North Korea understand that we stand with the South Koreans.

Mr. DAVIES. It is job one for us. That is correct.

Mr. BERA. Absolutely.

Mr. CHABOT. Thank you very much. The gentleman's time has expired. That is the end of the questioning this afternoon. We want to sincerely thank our panel, Ambassador Davies and Ambassador King for your testimony this afternoon. Members will have 5 days to revise their statements or submit questions in writing and if there is no further business to come before the committee, we are adjourned.

[Whereupon, at 3:20 p.m., the subcommittee was adjourned.]

APPENDIX

MATERIAL SUBMITTED FOR THE RECORD

SUBCOMMITTEE HEARING NOTICE
COMMITTEE ON FOREIGN AFFAIRS
U.S. HOUSE OF REPRESENTATIVES
WASHINGTON, DC 20515-6128

Subcommittee on Asia and the Pacific
Steve Chabot (R-OH), Chairman

July 14, 2014

TO: MEMBERS OF THE COMMITTEE ON FOREIGN AFFAIRS

You are respectfully requested to attend an OPEN hearing of the Committee on Foreign Affairs, to be held by the Subcommittee on Asia and the Pacific in Room 2172 of the Rayburn House Office Building (and available live on the Committee website at www.foreignaffairs.house.gov):

DATE: Wednesday, July 30, 2014

TIME: 2:00 p.m.

SUBJECT: Twenty-Years of U.S. Policy on North Korea: From Agreed Framework to Strategic Patience

WITNESSES: The Honorable Glyn Davies
Special Representative for North Korea Policy
Bureau of East Asian and Pacific Affairs
U.S. Department of State

The Honorable Robert King
Special Envoy for North Korean Human Rights
Office of the Special Envoy for Human Rights in North Korea
U.S. Department of State

By Direction of the Chairman

The Committee on Foreign Affairs seeks to make its facilities accessible to persons with disabilities. If you are in need of special accommodations, please call 202/225-5021 at least four business days in advance of the event, whenever practicable. Questions with regard to special accommodations in general (including availability of Committee materials in alternative formats and assistive listening devices) may be directed to the Committee.

COMMITTEE ON FOREIGN AFFAIRS

MINUTES OF SUBCOMMITTEE ON _____ *Asia & the Pacific* _____ HEARING

Day___*Wednesday*___Date_____*7/30/2014*_____Room_____*2172*_____

Starting Time ___*2:00 p.m.*___Ending Time ___*3:20 p.m.*___

Recesses |_____| (_____to_____) (_____to_____) (_____to_____) (_____to_____) (_____to_____) (_____to_____)

Presiding Member(s)

Chairman Steve Chabot (R-OH)

Check all of the following that apply:

Open Session ☑︎   Electronically Recorded (taped) ☑︎
Executive (closed) Session ☐   Stenographic Record ☑︎
Televised ☑︎

TITLE OF HEARING:

Twenty-Years of U.S. Policy on North Korea: From Agreed Framework to Strategic Patience

SUBCOMMITTEE MEMBERS PRESENT:

Rep. Ami Bera (D-CA), Rep. Scott Perry (R-PA), Rep. Brad Sherman (D-CA), Gerald Connolly (D-VA), George Holding (R-NC), Doug Collins (R-GA)

NON-SUBCOMMITTEE MEMBERS PRESENT: *(Mark with an * if they are not members of full committee.)*

HEARING WITNESSES: Same as meeting notice attached? Yes ☑︎ No ☐
(If "no", please list below and include title, agency, department, or organization.)

STATEMENTS FOR THE RECORD: *(List any statements submitted for the record.)*

TIME SCHEDULED TO RECONVENE _____
or
TIME ADJOURNED ___*3:20 p.m.*___

_____
Subcommittee Staff Director